SUPER
SANDCASTLE™
Let's Learn A to Z

Alcatraz to Zanzibar

Famous Places from A to Z

Colleen Dolphin

Consulting Editor, Diane Craig, M.A./Reading Specialist

ABDO
Publishing Company

Published by ABDO Publishing Company, 8000 West 78th Street, Edina, Minnesota 55439. Copyright © 2009 by Abdo Consulting Group, Inc. International copyrights reserved in all countries. No part of this book may be reproduced in any form without written permission from the publisher. Super SandCastle™ is a trademark and logo of ABDO Publishing Company.

Printed in the United States.

Editor: Martha E. H. Rustad
Content Developer: Nancy Tuminelly
Cover and Interior Design and Production: Colleen Dolphin, Mighty Media
Photo Credits: Linda Juntti, Shutterstock

Library of Congress Cataloging-in-Publication Data

Dolphin, Colleen, 1979-
   Alcatraz to Zanzibar : famous places from A to Z / Colleen Dolphin.
      p. cm. -- (Let's learn A to Z)
   ISBN 978-1-60453-492-4
   1. Geography--Juvenile literature. I. Title.

G175.D65 2009

910.3--dc22

                        2008023868

Super SandCastle™ books are created by a team of professional educators, reading specialists, and content developers around five essential components— phonemic awareness, phonics, vocabulary, text comprehension, and fluency— to assist young readers as they develop reading skills and strategies and increase their general knowledge. All books are written, reviewed, and leveled for guided reading, early reading intervention, and Accelerated Reader® programs for use in shared, guided, and independent reading and writing activities to support a balanced approach to literacy instruction.

About Super SandCastle™

Bigger Books for Emerging Readers
Grades K–4

Created for library, classroom, and at-home use, Super SandCastle™ books support and engage young readers as they develop and build literacy skills and will increase their general knowledge about the world around them. Super SandCastle™ books are part of SandCastle™, the leading preK–3 imprint for emerging and beginning readers. Super SandCastle™ features a larger trim size for more reading fun.

Let Us Know

Super SandCastle™ would like to hear your stories about reading this book. What was your favorite page? Was there something hard that you needed help with? Share the ups and downs of learning to read. We want to hear from you! Send us an e-mail.

sandcastle@abdopublishing.com

Contact us for a complete list of SandCastle™, Super SandCastle™, and other nonfiction and fiction titles from ABDO Publishing Company.

www.abdopublishing.com • 8000 West 78th Street Edina, MN 55439 • 800-800-1312 • 952-831-1632 fax

This fun and informative series employs illustrated definitions to introduce emerging readers to an alphabet of words in various topic areas. Each page combines words with corresponding images and descriptive sentences to encourage learning and knowledge retention. AlphagalorZ inspires young readers to find out more about the subjects that most interest them!

The "Guess what?" feature expands the reading and learning experience by offering additional information and fascinating facts about specific words or concepts. The "More Words" section provides additional related A to Z vocabulary words that develop and increase reading comprehension.

These books are appropriate for library, classroom, and home use.

Aa

Alcatraz

Alcatraz is an island off the coast of San Francisco, California. A prison was built on the island and was used from 1934 to 1963.

Guess what?

Alcatraz is also called "The Rock."

4

Big Ben

The bell in this tall clock tower in London, England, is known as Big Ben. It is about 150 years old.

Guess what?

The minute hand on the clock tower is 14 feet (4 m) long!

Chichén Itzá

Chichén Itzá is an ancient city in Mexico. The Mayas settled there because the land was good for planting crops.

Guess what?

Kulkulkan's Pyramid is one of the buildings in the city. It is 79 feet (24 m) tall.

Cc

Dead Sea

The Dead Sea is on the border between Israel and Jordan. It is even saltier than the ocean.

Guess what?

It's easy to float in the Dead Sea because the water is so salty.

Dd

Empire State Building

The Empire State Building is in New York City. It was finished in 1931 and was the world's tallest building until 1970.

Guess what?

It was built by about 3,400 people in only 410 days.

Ee

8

Fiji

Ff

Fiji is a country in the South Pacific Ocean. It is a group of more than 800 islands and islets.

Guess what?

People live on about 100 of Fiji's Islands.

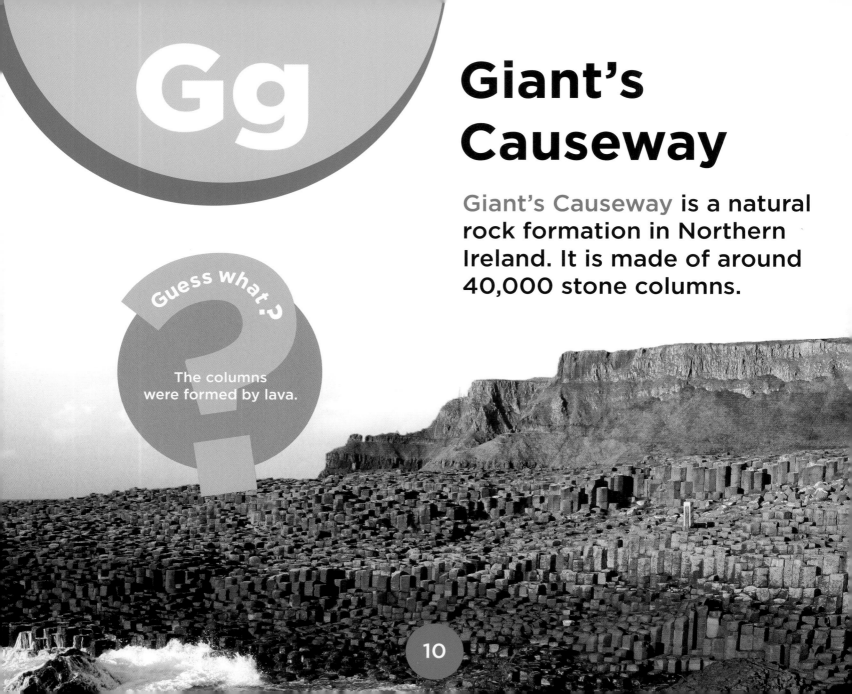

Gg

Giant's Causeway

Giant's Causeway is a natural rock formation in Northern Ireland. It is made of around 40,000 stone columns.

Guess what?

?

The columns were formed by lava.

Guess what?

The Himalayas are home to many different animals, such as tigers, yaks, and monkeys.

Himalayas

The Himalayas are the world's highest mountain range. They go across the nations of Bhutan, China, India, Nepal, Pakistan, and Afghanistan.

11

Hh

Ii

Istanbul

Istanbul is a city in Turkey. It is the only city in the world that is on both the European and Asian continents.

Guess what?

The Hagia Sophia is nearly 1,500 years old. It was a cathedral, then a mosque, and now it is a museum.

Jamaica

Jamaica is a small island country in the Caribbean Sea. **Jamaica** has mountains, valleys, plains, and beaches.

Jj

Guess what?

YS Falls is on the south coast of Jamaica.

Kuala Lumpur

Kuala Lumpur is the capital city of Malaysia. The Petronas Twin Towers in Kuala Lumpur are 1,483 feet (452 m) high.

Guess what?

These towers are the tallest twin buildings in the world!

Kk

Lake Baikal

Lake Baikal is in Siberia, Russia. It holds 20 percent of the world's freshwater.

Guess what?
More than 330 rivers and streams empty into Lake Baikal.

Machu Picchu

Machu Picchu is the ruins of an ancient city in Peru. The Incas built this city hundreds of years ago.

Mm

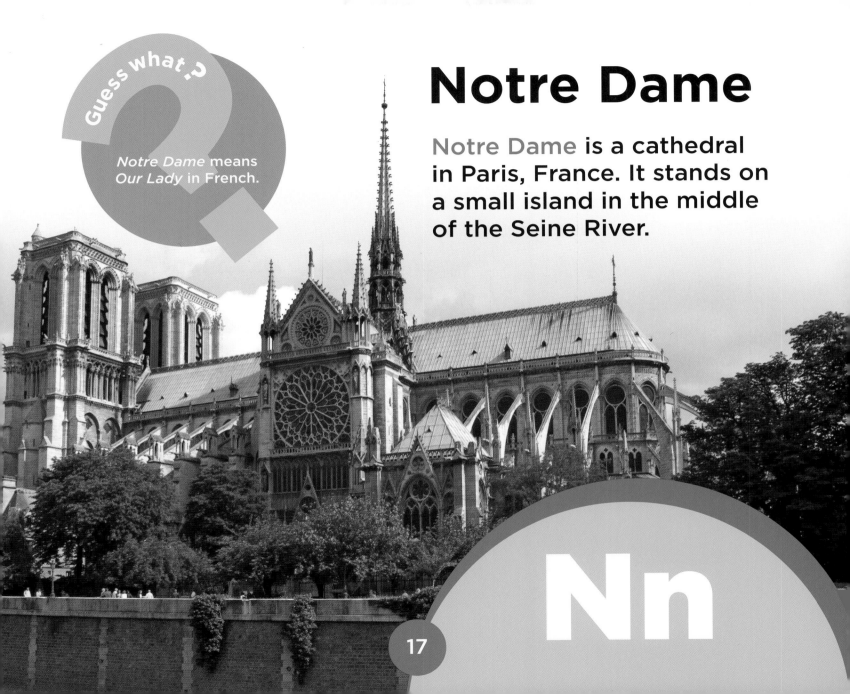

Guess what?

Notre Dame means *Our Lady* in French.

Notre Dame

Notre Dame is a cathedral in Paris, France. It stands on a small island in the middle of the Seine River.

Nn

17

Oo

Orkney

Guess what?

In Orkney there are more than 18 hours of daylight each day in June.

Orkney is a group of about 70 small islands off the coast of Scotland. People have lived on the Orkney Islands for more than 5,000 years.

Pompeii

Pompeii was a city in Italy thousands of years ago. It was covered in ash from the volcano Mount Vesuvius.

Guess what?

One survivor named Pliny the Younger wrote about the eruption of the volcano.

19

Qq

Qin Tomb

The Qin Tomb was built for the Chinese emperor Qin Shi Huangdi. He was buried with a life-size army made out of clay.

Guess what?

There are more than 7,000 clay statues in the Qin Tomb.

20

Red Square

Red Square is in Moscow, Russia. It has been a meeting place for Russians for thousands of years.

Guess what?

Red Square is *Krasnaya Ploshchad* in Russian. *Krasnaya* also means *beautiful*.

Rr

21

Sphinx

The Great Sphinx of Giza is in Egypt. It has a human head and the body of a lion. It was carved out of limestone.

Guess what.?

Some experts think the Sphinx was made to guard the Giza Plateau.

Ss

Taj Mahal

The Taj Mahal is in India.
It is a tomb that was built
for an emperor's wife.
It is surrounded by gardens.

Tt

Guess what?

People used more than
1,000 elephants to help
build Taj Mahal.

Uluru Rock

Uluru is a huge sandstone rock in Australia. The rock appears to change color as the light changes outside.

Guess what?

Uluru is also known as Ayers Rock.

Uu

24

Vancouver

Vancouver is in British Columbia. Many ships bring goods from Vancouver to other places.

Vv

Ww

Warsaw

Warsaw is the capital of Poland. It has many historic buildings.

Guess what?

The Old Town in Warsaw had to be rebuilt after World War II.

26

Xx

Xi River

The Xi River is in Southern China. It is used to carry goods by boat to different cities.

Guess what?

The Xi River is about 1,200 miles (1,931 km) long.

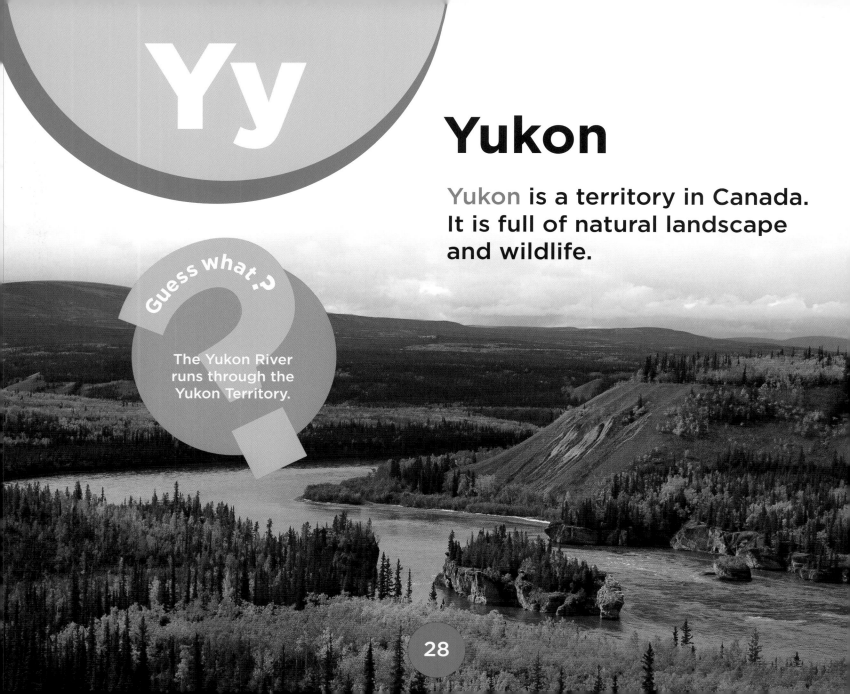

Yy

Yukon

Yukon is a territory in Canada. It is full of natural landscape and wildlife.

Guess what?

The Yukon River runs through the Yukon Territory.

28

Zanzibar

Zanzibar is an island
in the Indian Ocean.
It is part of the United
Republic of Tanzania.
Zanzibar has a tropical
climate and gets 60 to 80
inches (150 to 200 cm)
of rain each year.

Guess what?

Some of the animals
on Zanzibar include
leopards, monkeys,
mongooses, and
African pigs.

Zz

29

Glossary

ancient – very long ago or very old.

cathedral – a big, important church.

causeway – a road or path above wet ground.

climate – the usual weather in a place.

column – a narrow pillar.

continent – one of seven large land masses on earth. The continents are Asia, Africa, Europe, North America, South America, Australia, and Antarctica.

emperor – the ruler of an empire.

eruption – when lava and ashes shoot out of a volcano.

expert – a person very knowledgeable about a certain subject.

formation – the arrangement of things.

freshwater – water that is not salty, such as a lake or river.

goods – items that are bought and sold.

historic – being an important or famous part of history.

islet – a tiny island.

landscape – a large area of scenery.

lava – hot, melted rock from inside a volcano.

prison – a place where people who have committed crimes are locked up.

sandstone – made of sand held together by natural cement.

survivor – someone who lives through a bad experience, such as a flood, fire, or illness.

tomb – a place where someone is buried.

tropical – located in the hottest areas on earth.

twin – one of two objects that are the same.

volcano – a mountain that has lava and ash inside of it.

wildlife – wild mammals, birds, and fish living in their natural habitat.

More Famous Places!

Can you learn about these famous places too?

Alamo	Great Wall of China	Nairobi
Angel Falls	Harbor of Rio de Janeiro	Netherlands
Acropolis	Heaven's Tower	Nova Scotia
Berlin Wall	Hollywood	Palau
Belem Tower	Hong Kong	Paracutin Volcano
Ben Navis	Hoover Dam	Panama Canal
Bermuda Triangle	Hotel del Coronado	Ponte Vecchio
Coliseum	Itaipu Dam	Price Edward Island
Corkscrew Canyon	Iditarod	Qatar
Cairo	Innsbruck	Rome
Cyprus	Japan	Shanghai
DisneyWorld	Kenya	Statue of Liberty
Duomo Cathedral	Kennedy Space Center	Stonehenge
Eiffel Tower	Kinkakuji	Suez Canal
Everglades	Leaning Tower of Pisa	Sydney Opera House
Fiji Islands	Lighthouse of Alexandria	Venice
Forbidden City	Louvre Museum	Versailles
Galapagos Islands	Mount Everest	Washington, D.C.
Golden Gate Bridge	Mount Kilimanjaro	Wailing Wall in Jerusalem
Graceland	Mount Rushmore	Yellowstone National Park
Grand Canyon	Mount St. Helens	Yemen
Grand Palace	New York City	Zurich
Great Barrier Reef	Niagara Falls	Zephyr Cove